Welcome and thank you for choosing
this unique piece of work!

Before you start the adventure of
coloring this book, remember this;
DO NO THINK, be here, Observe
the harmony in the details of each
drawing, let the world of the
imagination consume you and just go
for it.

Please do not use markers or alcohol
based markers as their ink may bleed
slightly due to paper thickness.
Crayons, stencils, or fine tip
washable markers work the best.

INFINITISM II

LOVERS AND DREAMERS

By artist Juan Pablo Zapata

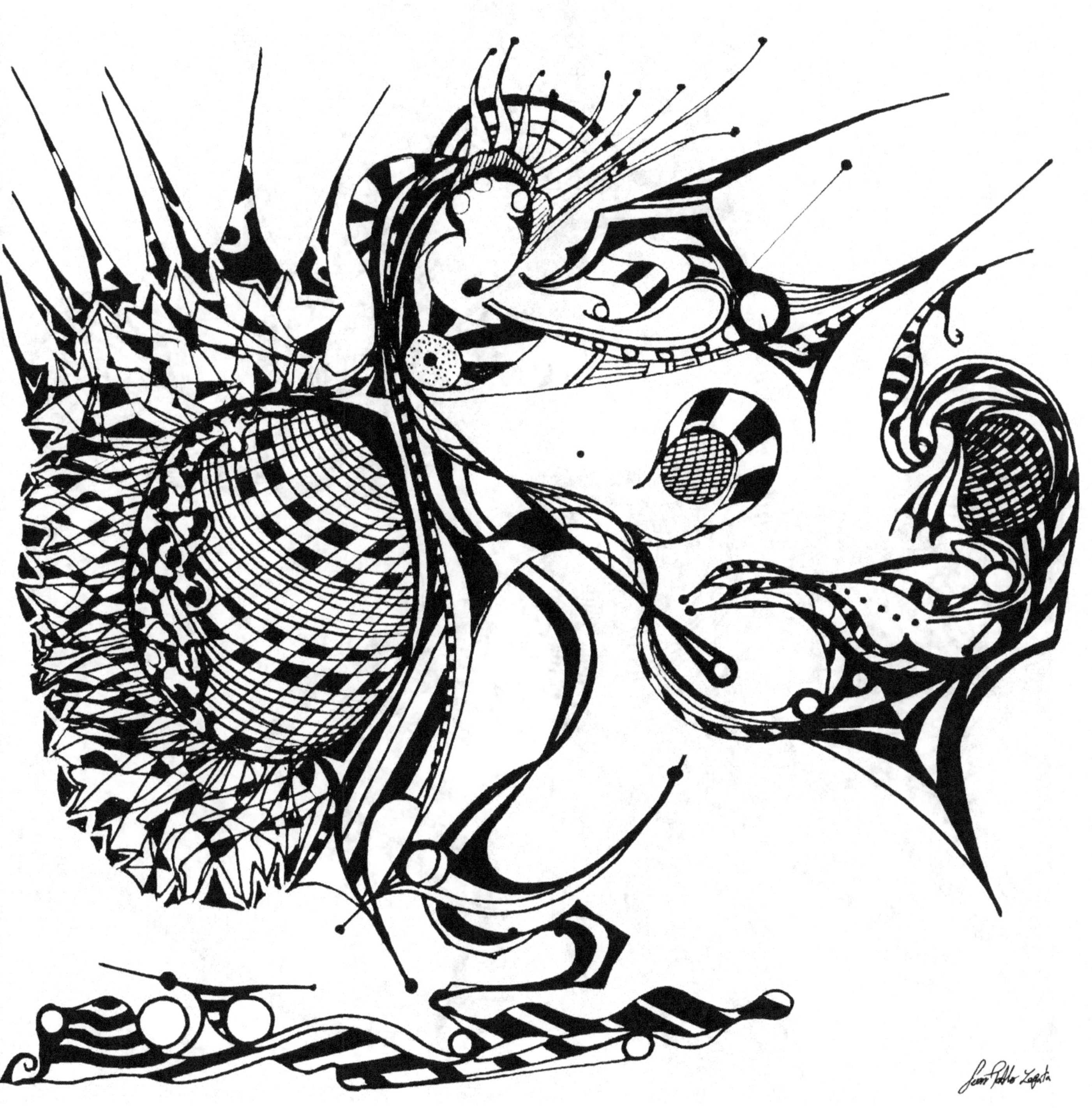

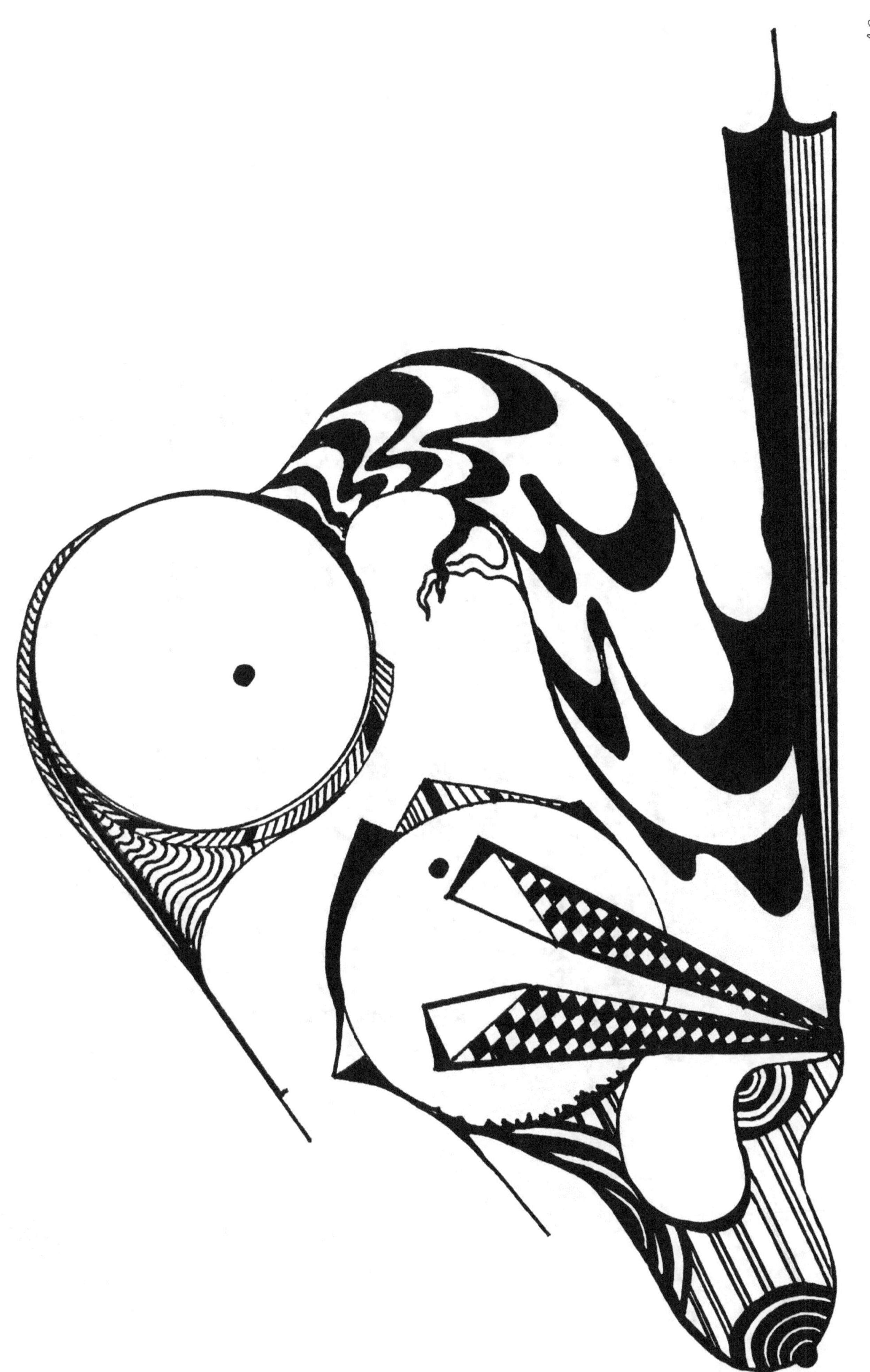

"Darkness is just the shadow of light".

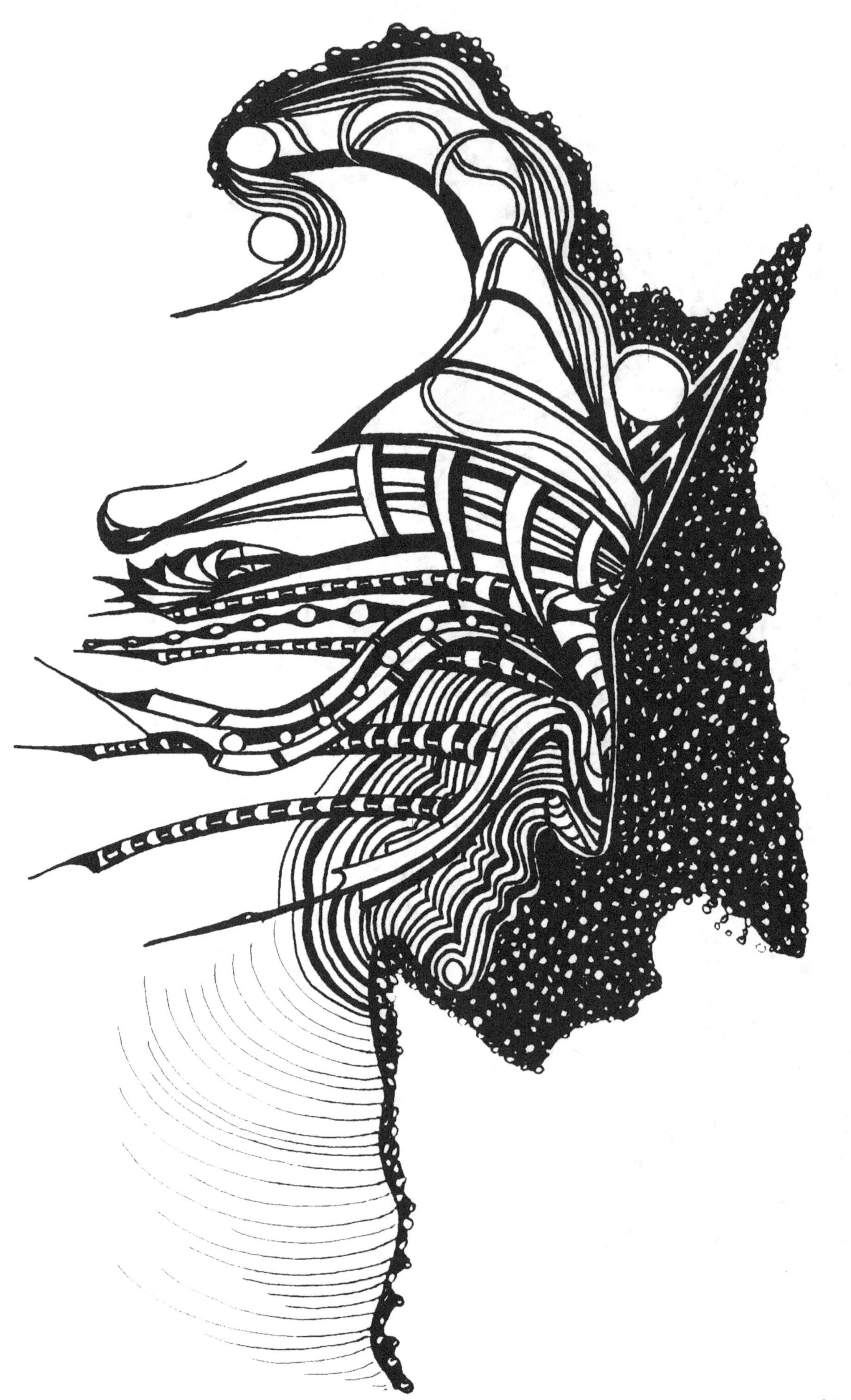

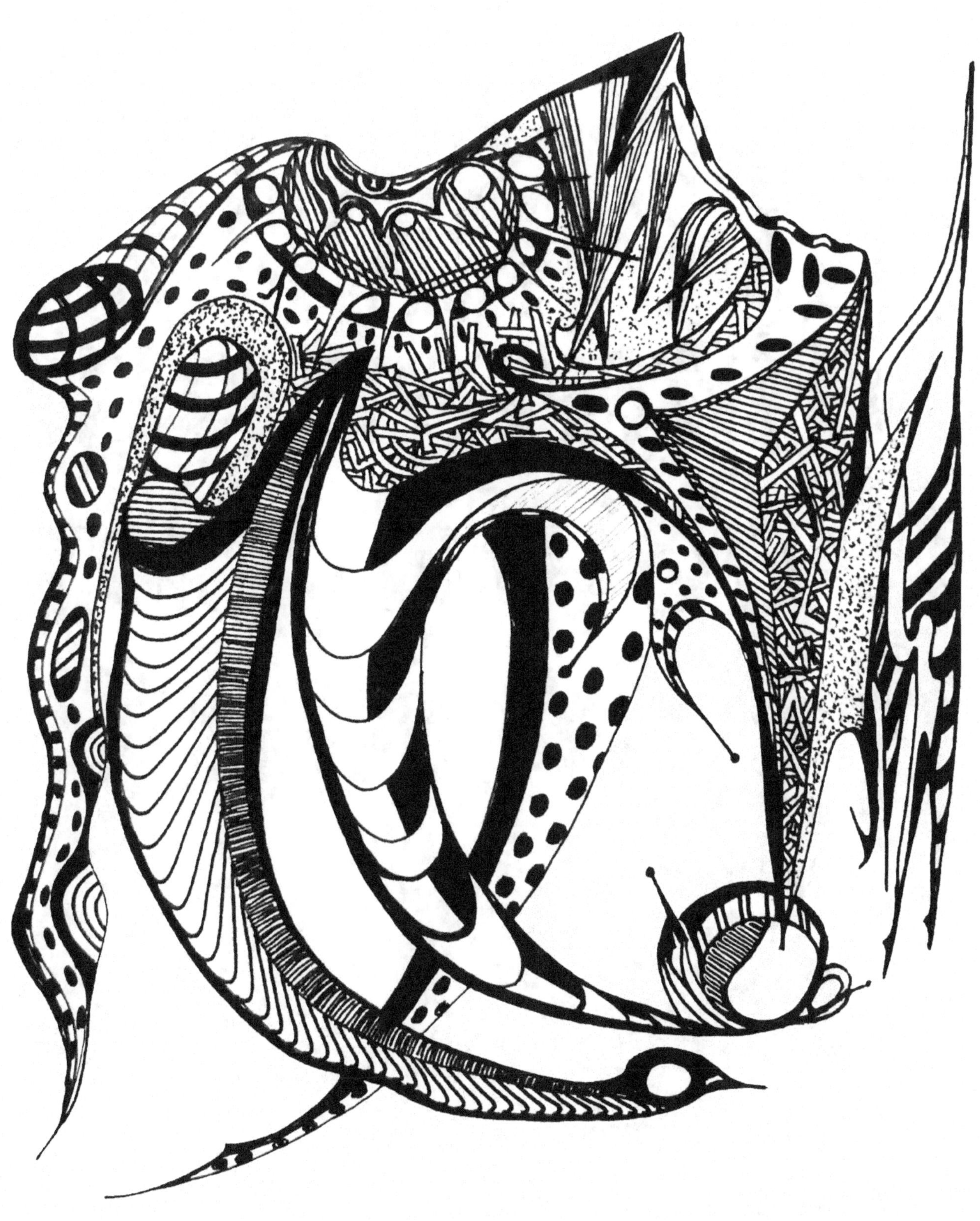

"There is nothing but freedom in creating".

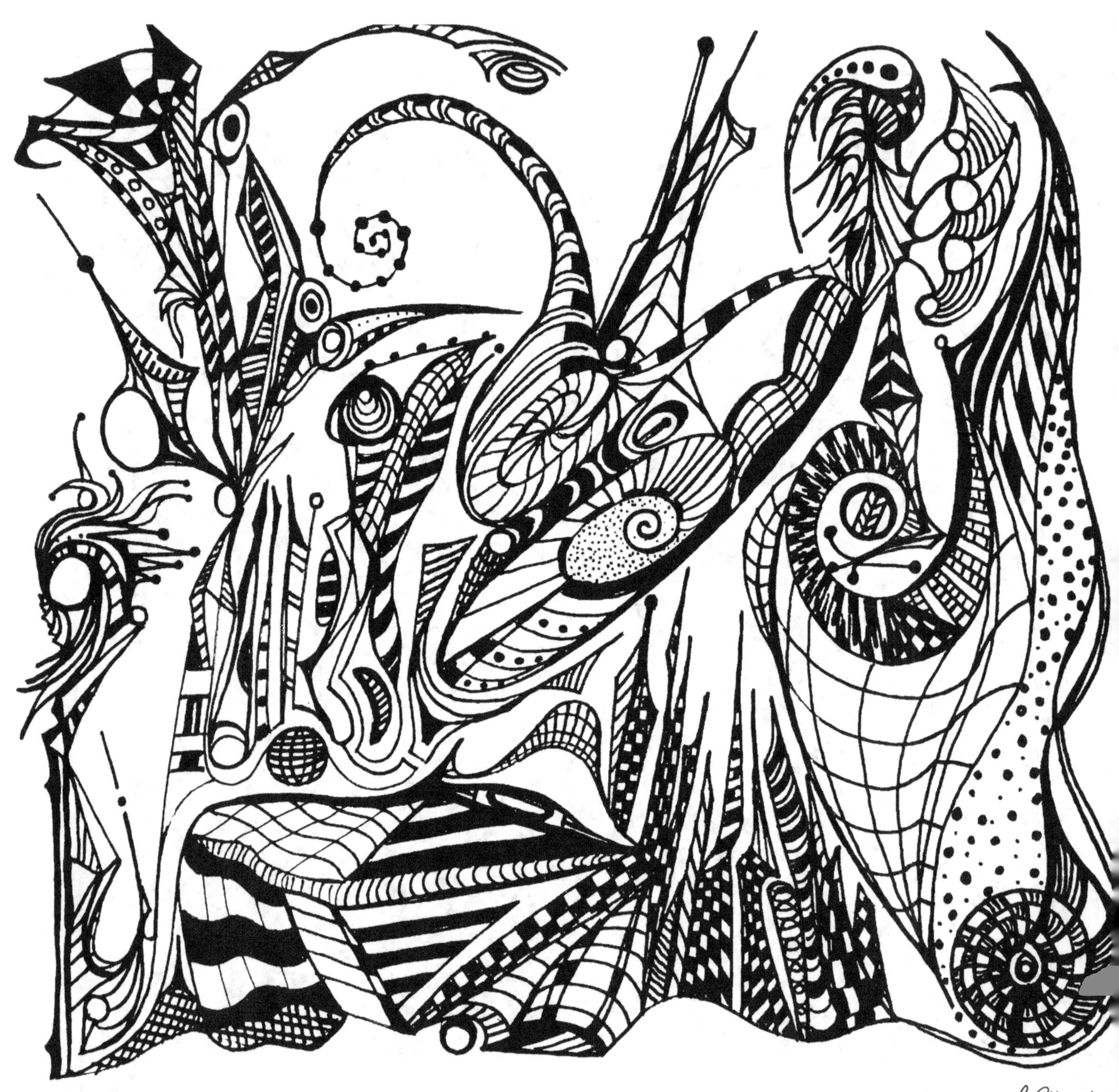

Artist: Juan Pablo Zapata

www.zapata.studio